Keanu Reeves

A Little Golden Book® Biography

By Emily Easton • Illustrated by Olga Lee

A GOLDEN BOOK • NEW YORK

Golden Books
An imprint of Random House Children's Books • A division of Penguin Random House LLC
1745 Broadway, New York, NY 10019 • penguinrandomhouse.com • rhcbooks.com
Text copyright © 2025 by Emily Easton
Cover art and interior illustrations copyright © 2025 by Olga Lee
Golden Books, A Golden Book, A Little Golden Book, the G colophon, and the distinctive
gold spine are registered trademarks of Penguin Random House LLC.
Library of Congress Control Number: 2024949988
ISBN 978-0-593-80796-5 (trade) — ISBN 978-0-593-80797-2 (ebook)
Manufactured in the United States of America
10 9 8 7 6 5 4 3 2 1
The authorized representative in the EU for product safety and compliance is Penguin
Random House Ireland, Morrison Chambers, 32 Nassau Street, Dublin D02 YH68, Ireland,
https://eu-contact.penguin.ie.

Keanu Charles Reeves was born on September 2, 1964, in Beirut, Lebanon. His parents named him Keanu, which means "cool breeze over the mountains" in Hawaiian, to honor his father's Chinese Hawaiian heritage.

Soon after, the family moved to Sydney, Australia, where his sister Kim was born.

When Keanu was still a toddler, his parents' marriage ended. Keanu, Kim, and their mom moved to New York City to start over. His mom got married again, this time to movie director Paul Aaron. Their marriage didn't last, but Keanu's stepfather Paul stayed in his life even after his family moved to Toronto, Canada, when Keanu was seven.

In Toronto, his mother worked as a costume designer for famous rock stars. Keanu would clean her studio on weekends to earn money.

When Keanu was twelve years old, his mother married a third time, and his sister Karina was born.

Keanu's family moved around a lot in Toronto. Always being the new kid at school was hard. So Keanu escaped to the movies, and he soon discovered the theater. He loved acting and playing different characters.

A local community theater gave him the perfect place to put on a show and many new friends to do it with. His performance in a small role in *Romeo and Juliet* caught the eye of a talent agent. Acting jobs in commercials and Canadian TV shows soon followed.

One summer vacation, Paul let Keanu work as an assistant on the set of the movie he was directing. Keanu carried ice and drinks for the actors and helped with other small tasks. He watched closely and learned how films were made. The teamwork between the actors and the crew was his favorite part.

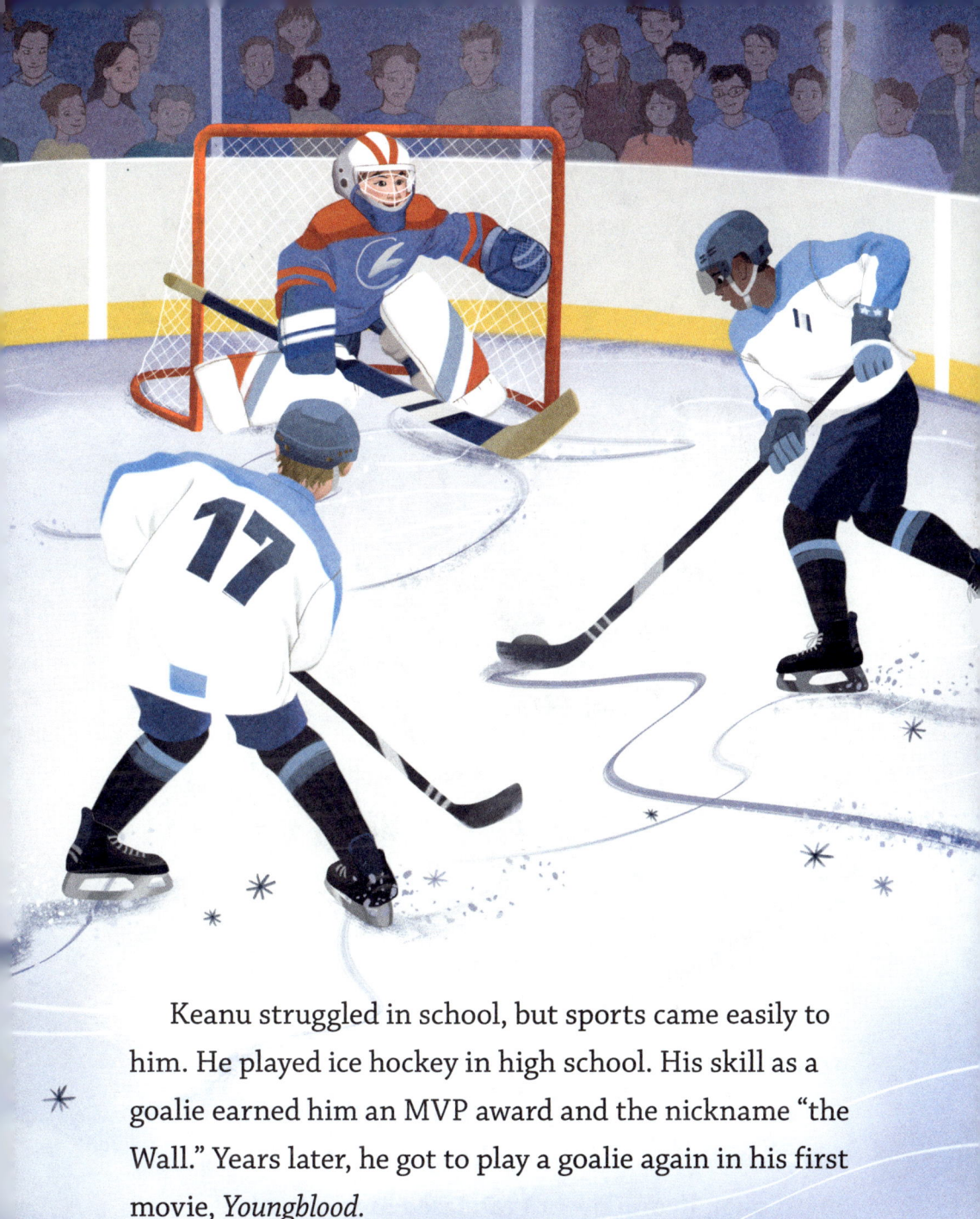

Keanu struggled in school, but sports came easily to him. He played ice hockey in high school. His skill as a goalie earned him an MVP award and the nickname "the Wall." Years later, he got to play a goalie again in his first movie, *Youngblood*.

Keanu went to four different high schools in five years. The last school focused on the performing arts, which seemed perfect for the budding actor. But Keanu had a hard time fitting in—and following the rules. Even though he would always continue reading and learning on his own, Keanu never graduated high school.

Instead, he signed up for theater classes to focus on becoming a better actor.

When he was twenty years old, Keanu felt ready for bigger things. He packed up his car and drove from Toronto to Los Angeles, where Paul helped him pursue his Hollywood dream.

After a few years of small parts in commercials, TV shows, and movies, Keanu finally made it big. In 1989, he starred in the hit movie *Bill and Ted's Excellent Adventure*, about two best friends who travel through time in a phone booth so they can pass their history test and save the world.

These air-guitar-playing "dudes"—who used California surfer slang for some of their "most excellent" lines—were sweet but not so bright, and many fans confused Keanu with Ted, his clueless character.

Keanu chose to ignore the "bogus" criticism. He focused on working with talented people he could learn from and continued to "party on," as Ted would say.

In 1991, Keanu put down his air guitar to play a real
bass guitar in the band Dogstar, which he formed with a
drummer he met in a grocery store checkout line. The
band recorded albums and toured the world in between
Keanu's busy moviemaking schedule.

Keanu continued to stretch himself as an actor, starring in comedies, dramas, and action-filled thrillers. But fame was never his goal.

He just loved acting—especially in plays written by William Shakespeare. He even turned down the chance to star in the sequel to his hit action movie *Speed* so he could play the lead in *Hamlet* in a small Canadian theater.

In 1999, Keanu made a film that changed moviemaking forever. The special effects and action scenes of *The Matrix* looked different from every other movie.

Keanu trained hard to prepare to play the character Neo. He spent more time learning martial arts than it took to make the entire movie!

Speed isn't just the title of one of Keanu's hit action movies—he loves going fast in real life, too! He learned to surf for his movie *Point Break*. And he got lessons from a race car driver so he could do his own driving stunts in the *John Wick* movies

But his real love is riding motorcycles, a joy he shares
with the *Toy Story 4* character he voiced, Duke Caboom.
He even gave stunt actors from *The Matrix* their own
motorcycles to thank them for
their work!

When he's not performing, Keanu enjoys living a
quiet life away from Hollywood. Because he is so private,
people get excited whenever they catch a glimpse of him.
A photo of Keanu eating alone on a park bench inspired
fans to add funny captions and images to their own
versions of Sad Keanu and share it on the internet. This
is called a meme—and Keanu memes are very popular!

Fans also love seeing videos of Keanu being a down-to-earth, helpful guy—like when he gave up his seat to a fellow passenger on the New York City subway or when he shared a van ride to LA with other stranded airplane travelers. But Keanu doesn't think he's doing anything special. Like Bill and Ted, he believes we should all "be excellent to each other."

Keanu helps people in small ways and in very big ways. He donated millions of dollars to cancer research and children's hospitals and has raised money for SCORE—a group that helps support people living with spinal cord injuries.

Keanu is more popular than ever—and so are his films. He continues to work hard to be the best actor he can be. And he wants to keep going until he makes one hundred movies or more! That's great news for his fans.

Party on, Keanu!